EVERYBODY'S GUIDE TO PUNCTUATION

EVERYBODY'S
GUIDE TO
PUNCTUATION

By
HAROLD HERD

London
GEORGE ALLEN & UNWIN LTD
RUSKIN HOUSE MUSEUM STREET

FIRST PUBLISHED MARCH 1925
SECOND IMPRESSION NOVEMBER 1925
THIRD IMPRESSION APRIL 1929
FOURTH IMPRESSION 1932
FIFTH IMPRESSION 1938
SIXTH IMPRESSION 1952
SEVENTH IMPRESSION 1962
EIGHTH IMPRESSION 1969

SBN 04 421001 9

PRINTED BY Unwin Brothers Limited
THE GRESHAM PRESS OLD WOKING SURREY ENGLAND

Produced by Letterpress

A member of the Staples Printing Group   (HL 3576)

PREFACE

THE aim of this work is to provide a simple explanation of the modern rules of punctuation.

The passing of the more formal style of prose has been accompanied by the discarding of those rules of punctuation which checked the flow of expression. Stops are now rarely suffered to cramp the writer's ideas; the reader is spared the jolts and jerks of mechanical pointing.

When punctuation was first employed, it was in the rôle of the handmaid of prose; later the handmaid was transformed by the pedants into a harsh-faced chaperone, pervertedly ingenious in the contriving of stiff regulations and starched rules of decorum ; now, happily, she is content to act as an auxiliary to the writer and as a guide to the reader.

HAROLD HERD.

CONTENTS

EVERYBODY'S GUIDE TO PUNCTUATION

THE ORIGIN OF PUNCTUATION

THINK what a repellent jumble the printed page would be if it were entirely devoid of stops : the reading of a newspaper or a book would be a continuous strain.

Yet books were once written without any stops to aid the reader. What is difficult to conceive is that at one time words were not even separated from one another. The first MSS. had no devices of any kind to lighten the reader's labour. Words followed one after the other without a distinguishing space ; the reader had to decipher long strings of letters rather than to read lines of words.

The first step towards punctuation was taken when someone thought of leaving spaces between the words ; then came the introduction of full stops ; and finally, a system of pointing was evolved.

In these days we take punctuation for granted, so much so that little curiosity has been felt with regard to the origin of the art of pointing.   Other benefactors of the human race have been honoured in song or story, but the men who have made easier the path of many generations of readers are almost unknown.

Aristophanes of Byzantium is credited with the devising of a system of punctuation in the third century B.C.   A single point was variously placed to denote the pauses now marked by the full stop, comma and semicolon.   This system was not widely employed, however, and for many centuries no method of punctuation was generally observed.

The name of Aldus Manutius is known

to bibliophiles as that of an early printer who produced work of rare excellence, but he has a further claim to fame for his service to literature by the introduction in the sixteenth century of a system of pointing.

Once a puzzle picture even to the learned, the written word is now quickly assimilable by anyone of average intelligence.

THE PURPOSE OF PUNCTUATION

THE main purpose of punctuation is to assist the writer to make a clear impression on the reader's mind. It enables him to convey his meaning more swiftly and exactly than would be possible if no stops were inserted.

Punctuation should not be looked upon as a substitute for clear expression; it is merely an aid to the immediate comprehension of the writer's meaning. Stops are not intended as crutches to support limping sentence constructions. A good writer searches for the simplest and most vivid way of expressing an idea, and uses punctuation solely to communicate that idea instantly and with fitting emphasis on the various parts of his message.

Over-stopping clogs the flow of expression, and is almost invariably the accompaniment of a heavy style. Often a writer defeats his purpose because he ignores the effect of punctuation on the pace of his sentences. Let us suppose that he wants to rouse his readers to passionate sympathy with his cause : is it not obvious that he will fail to stir their emotions if his writing is burdened with stops ? Their sympathy will not be fired by closely punctuated and consequently dragging sentences.

Stops do the work that their name implies : they mark the stops or halts on the way. They should be inserted only at the natural pauses, or to avoid obscurity ; if they are used too frequently they give the page a jumpy appearance and create an effect of jerkiness on the reader's mind.

Without the help of punctuation absolute precision would be impossible in many cases. Notice the difference of meaning conveyed by the use of extra stops in the following :—

> It is not true I told him.
> " It is not true," I told him.

The former version implies that it was not true that the speaker told something to someone ; the correct punctuation reveals the intended meaning. In speech the inflection of the voice prevents misunderstanding in such a case. Deprived of the aid of gesture and the infinite gradations of the voice, the writer has to get his effects with the pen and use stops to show the relation of one part of a sentence to another.

A missing or a wrongly-inserted stop may be the cause of an unfortunate misapprehension or actual loss ; usually it results merely in ambiguity or absurdity. The insertion of a wrong stop cost the United States about two million dollars many years ago. A section of a Tariff Bill enumerated the articles to be admitted free of duty, among them being " all foreign fruit-plants," which denoted plants for propagation or experiment. In copying the bill a clerk accidentally changed the hyphen to a comma, and the wording then ran : " All foreign fruit, plants, etc." Until Congress could rectify the error, a year later, all foreign fruits were admitted free of duty.

THE MAIN RULES AT A GLANCE

THE COMMA denotes a short pause, or is inserted to make the meaning instantly clear.

THE SEMICOLON marks a longer pause. It is mainly used to separate parts of a sentence that are too closely related to be made into distinct sentences.

THE COLON, which indicates a more abrupt pause, is chiefly used now-adays to introduce quotations and enumerations.

THE FULL STOP marks the end of a sentence.

THE MARK OF INTERROGATION, commonly known as the question mark, is placed after a direct question.

THE MARK OF EXCLAMATION is placed after interjections and exclamatory expressions.

THE DASH denotes that a phrase is incomplete. It also serves several miscellaneous purposes.

THE HYPHEN joins two words together.

INVERTED COMMAS enclose direct quotations.

THE APOSTROPHE indicates the possessive case.

HOW TO PUNCTUATE

THE COMMA

THE comma is inserted

(*a*) To denote a short pause in the sentence.

> Throughout the day birthday presents had been arriving, and an old servant, grey-haired and bent, had been given the task of opening the packages.

(*b*) After nouns, pronouns or adjectives, when a series of such words is used.

> On treatment by destructive distillation in a retort, the Somerset shale yielded oil, gas, ammonia, water and a residue called shale

ash. (It will be observed that the comma has been omitted after " water." Current usage supports the omission when the last word of a series is preceded by a conjunction, e.g., " and ", as in this case.)

She spoke in a low, pleasant, cultivated voice.

(*c*) To mark off words used in apposition (a grammatical term chiefly used to denote the addition of one noun to another).

William Ewart Gladstone, the great statesman, declared on one occasion . . . etc.

Abraham Lincoln, America's best-beloved president, was one of the homeliest men who ever ruled a great nation.

(*d*) To mark the vocative case (i.e., the case used in addressing a person or a thing).

No, sir.

(*e*) Before   and   after   explanatory phrases.

> The new plan, on the whole, is better fitted to meet the need.

(*f*) After adverbs such as further, however, etc., when they begin a sentence, and before and after when they occur in the middle of a sentence.

> Further, we must have regard to the possible consequences.
>
> It was almost immediately seen, however, that the measure would meet with stern opposition.

(*g*) To separate the parts of a sentence.

> The ordinary eye could not catch the fine shades of expression in the eyes, in the arched eyebrows, in the lifting slant of the forehead with its one deep wrinkle, or in the great

mouth hidden behind the great black moustache.

(*h*) Before and after words or phrases that check the progress of the sentence.

It was not to be expected, he remarked, that they would assent to this proposal.

There has been a tendency, the report proceeded, to interfere with the working of the scheme, and later, to ostracise its supporters. (Some writers would prefer to enclose " the report proceeded " between parenthesis, and this method is equally permissible.)

(*i*) To denote the omission of words.

Thomas Hardy has immortalised Wessex, and Arnold Bennett, the Five Towns.

(*j*) Before (or after) words enclosed by inverted commas.

> He said, " I will not see this man."
> " I am expecting to receive a letter any moment," he added.

(*k*) After each group of three consecutive figures in a number, counting from the right.

> 29,487.
> 1,424,931.
> 109,623,586.

THE SEMICOLON

(*a*) THE semicolon marks a longer pause than is indicated by the comma.

> His record commends him; his personality repels.
>
> The future lies in the balance; the theatre lies sick unto death.

(*b*) As a general rule it is used to separate parts of a sentence that are too closely related to be made into distinct sentences.

> Last year we had a precocious spring; this year we had a late one; but by this time last year's spring had suffered a fatal blight, and now the present spring has become laden with promise.

The Bill does not in itself answer any of these questions ; it makes it more necessary than ever to find an answer.

(*c*) It is used to separate points that are set out in specific form.

How the skill and intelligence needed for our industries is best recruited ; what part the maldistribution of labour plays in our present economic confusion ; how young workers can best be guided into the employments that suit them ; how the blind alley can be eliminated —these are all questions demanding the most careful inquiry.

THE COLON

THE colon

(*a*) Denotes a more abrupt pause than is marked by the semicolon, but is more commonly used nowadays for the purposes enumerated in (*b*) and (*c*).

> But yesterday the word of Cæsar might
> Have stood against the world : now lies he there,
> And none so poor to do him reverence.
> SHAKESPEARE.

> Thank you for your suggestions : they strike the right note.

(*b*) The colon is employed (with or without a dash) to introduce quotations.

He reminded them of the old proverb : " Charity begins at home, but should not end there."

The gist of his letter was contained in the words :—" The scheme is pure speculation."

(*c*) It is also employed (with or without a dash) before enumerations.

The following nations have agreed to participate : Britain, America, France and Italy.

The office contained the following articles :—A flat-top desk, a small table, two chairs, a small card-index cabinet and a faded carpet.

THE FULL STOP

(*a*) THE full stop (also known as the period and the full point) is used at the end of every sentence.

Time is a great governing factor.
The vice-president also supported the resolution, which was then put to the meeting and carried unanimously.

Exceptions to this rule are exclamatory and interrogative sentences, as explained in the sections on the use of the points of exclamation and interrogation.

(*b*) The full stop is employed after initial letters, abbreviations, and (but not generally) ordinal numbers written in Roman numerals.

W. E. Gladstone.
Rt. Hon. ; Rt. Rev.

A.D. 1924 ; M.A. ; MS. (singular) and MSS. (plural) ; Mr. ; i.e. and e.g. ; cwts. ; a.m. ; etc.

Edward II. ; Chapter XI.

(*c*) Numbers in lists of books, etc., are followed by the full point.

29. The Cloister and the Hearth.

THE MARK OF INTERROGATION

(*a*) THE note of interrogation or question mark is placed after a direct question.

> What explanation did he give ?
> Is there a short-cut to the village ?

(*b*) Each question takes the mark of interrogation, unless the questions require only one answer, as in the second of the following examples.

> Is this the usual practice ? Would it be equally acceptable in London and the provinces ? Are there purely local conditions anywhere ?
> Can you come up to town to-morrow, and meet us at the Hotel Splendide ?

(*c*) Indirect questions do not take the point of interrogation.

Direct.

" Is that the sole reason ? " he inquired.

Indirect.

He inquired whether that was the sole reason.

(*d*) As explained in the next section, the note of exclamation is used after sentences that are interrogative in construction, but really exclamatory.

(*e*) The mark of interrogation enclosed within brackets is occasionally employed to suggest a doubt as to the truth or aptness of a preceding word or phrase, or to indicate irony.

The new leader (?) will be put to the test this week.

THE MARK OF EXCLAMATION

(*a*) THE exclamation mark is placed after interjections and exclamatory expressions.

> Farewell, a long farewell to all my greatness !—SHAKESPEARE.

> Poverty ! thou source of human art,
> Thou great inspirer of the poet's song !—MOORE.

> Oh !
> Thou then would'st make mine enemy my judge !—SHELLEY.

> God save the King !
> Hark !
> Stand back !

(*b*) The note of exclamation is occasionally employed after ironical statements.

> I have read his autobiography. It is a story of uninterrupted success ; never did his vision fail him or his confidence falter. A modest man !

(*c*) The exclamation mark is used to heighten the effect of any statement that contains absurdity.

> He declared that he had discovered the secret of perpetual motion !

(*d*) A sentence that is interrogative in form but exclamatory in effect should be followed by the exclamation mark.

> How can you believe such a wild assertion !

THE DASH

(*a*) THE dash is used to show that something is left incomplete.

> What you say is true, but—
> The result was—well, you can readily picture what followed.

The full stop is omitted where the dash indicates an unfinished sentence, but it is permissible to use the note of interrogation or the note of exclamation.

> And then— ?
> Think of the consequences if— !

(*b*) Hesitancy in speech may be indicated by the dash.

> I hope so—but—that is—well, I will give it a trial.

(c) The dash is sometimes inserted before and after a parenthetical statement.

The year has been a record of continued progress—except for a curious set-back in July—and next year promises even bigger things.

(d) The dash is used to give more force to repetition.

If we are to get this plan adopted—if we are to carry the country with us—we must organise.

(e) The dash is occasionally employed to mark an impressive pause.

What is their present state? Homeless—starving—stricken with disease—plunged into awful despair.

(f) The side-heading of a paragraph should be followed by a full stop and

The Reference Department.—This department of the Public Library is rendering useful service to the community.

(*g*) A full stop and dash are also placed between a quotation and the name of the author, work or newspaper, when the source is given on the same line.

Better new friend than an old foe.—SPENSER.

THE HYPHEN

(*a*) THE hyphen is used to join two words together.

> Commander-in-Chief ; cream-laid ; hand-carved ; home-made ; rowing-boat.

Many compound words do not take a hyphen, but there is no rule governing the subject. The modern tendency is to join words without the use of the hyphen.

(*b*) The hyphen is placed between syllables that have the same vowel adjoining, to show that the two vowels are not to be pronounced together.

> Co-opt ; pre-empt ; re-elect.

(*c*) When using " re- " as a living prefix to a simple verb, a hyphen should be inserted to avoid confusion with a compound verb.

Re-cover ; re-create.

(*d*) The hyphen should be inserted when a prefix is placed before a proper name.

Pro-British ; pre-Christian.

(*e*) Several words are sometimes linked by hyphens.

The never-say-die party.
Go-as-you-please methods.

(*f*) When numbers are written in words, the hyphen is used to separate the component parts.

Twenty-five ; twenty-fifth ; eight-and-twenty ; nine-and-twentieth.

This rule applies also to fractional parts written in words.

Five-sixths ; five-fourteenths.

(*g*) " A " used as a prefix before **a** verbal noun ending in -ing is followed by **a** hyphen.

> A-sighing and a-sobbing.

(*h*) When **a** word is divided between two lines, the first part takes a hyphen. The division should be at the end of **a** syllable.

> Conjec-tured ; associa-tion ; statements ; re-ported.

BRACKETS

THERE are two kinds of brackets—the square [] and the curved (). The latter is better known as the parenthesis.

(*a*) When words that are not grammatically essential are introduced into a sentence they are enclosed within brackets. Dashes are sometimes employed in lieu of brackets, as explained in the section defining the uses of that point.

The design has points of resemblance with the Doge's Palace (and as Stockholm is known as the Venice of the North this is not inappropriate), but the style in which the parts are worked out is entirely original.

The question he asks (and only partly answers) is not so much " Where are we ? " as " Whither are we going ? "

Note that in the first example the comma follows the bracket, because the parenthesis belongs to that part of the sentence. The insertion of brackets is the only change in the punctuation of a sentence involved by the inclusion of a parenthesis.

(*b*) Brackets are occasionally employed to enclose an entire parenthetical sentence.

Our train arrived late at night. (Have I already told you that we had hoped to reach our destination by 3 o'clock in the afternoon ?) Our first glimpse of the town was blurred by drizzling rain.

(*c*) The modern tendency is to use curved brackets almost exclusively.   One use of the square bracket is to enclose any comment or explanation made by a writer while quoting a passage.

> One day Mr. Maxwell [the other candidate] and I wanted to go out hunting.

The square bracket is also employed to enclose conjectural missing words, e.g., words omitted from a hastily-written letter published in a biography, or words supplied to fill in the gap caused by part of a document having been torn off.

A further use of the square bracket is to enclose a parenthetical word or phrase that occurs within a parenthesis.

INVERTED COMMAS

(*a*) INVERTED commas (also known as " quotes ") are employed to enclose direct quotations, i.e., the actual words used by another person.

"What is the meaning of this uproar ? " he demanded.

It was Abraham Lincoln who said : " Government of the people, by the people, for the people."

(*b*) Any words occurring in an indirect sentence that are given in direct form should be denoted by inverted commas.

He remarked that the " bold originality " of this policy was not so apparent as its author believed.

An indirect quotation does not require inverted commas. Compare the following with the first example.

> He demanded to know the meaning of the uproar.

(*c*) A quotation within a quotation is enclosed within single inverted commas.

> He answered sharply : " Brown told me, ' I will let you have the report to-morrow.' "

Writers who make a practice of employing single inverted commas for quotations should reverse the foregoing rule.

(*d*) Slang expressions or words used in a sense differing from current usage are usually marked by inverted commas. In this way the writer shows that he is aware that the word is slang or that it is employed in a manner that does not conform to the best usage.

The fruit had a " moreish " flavour.

It was certainly an " ultra-smart " affair.

(*e*) The titles of books, plays and musical compositions ; the names of newspapers ; and the names of ships, should be enclosed within inverted commas or italicised.

The quotation is from Gray's " Elegy."

Last night's performance was of " The Tales of Hoffman."

I saw the advertisement in the " Daily Telegraph." (The names of newspapers are more commonly given in italics.)

The " Aquitania " arrived yesterday morning. (Names of ships are also frequently printed in italics.)

(*f*) If the quotation is interrogative or exclamatory in form, the point of inter-

rogation or exclamation should precede
the final pair of inverted commas.

> " What do they want ? " he
> inquired.
> His retort was expressed in a
> single word : " Never ! "

(*g*) If a sentence that is interrogative
or exclamatory in form ends with a
quotation, the appropriate point follows
the inverted commas.

> Was it not Emerson who said,
> " Self-trust is the first secret of
> success " ?
> And this was the " ideal village " !

(*h*) If an interrogative or exclamatory
sentence ends with a quotation that
contains a question or an exclamation,
the appropriate point is placed after the
inverted commas.

Do you remember the poet's question, " Can wealth bring happiness " ?

How we thrilled when we first heard the command to " Charge " !

NOTE.—Inverted commas are unnecessary when the quotation is printed in smaller type or indented (i.e., set back from the margin, similarly to the examples of punctuation given in this work); but any quotation occurring within such quotation needs the commas.

THE APOSTROPHE

(*a*) THE apostrophe denotes the possessive case of nouns. The letter " s " is added to singular nouns, and is preceded by the apostrophe.

> The lady's hat.
> The chairman's speech.

In order to avoid undue sibilance, it is usual not to add " 's " to some nouns (particularly ancient words) which end with that letter.

> Socrates' wisdom.

In words of one syllable " 's " may be added, but many writers prefer to omit it, especially in the much-discussed example of " St. James's Street."

In plural nouns the apostrophe follows the " s " that indicates the plural number.

> The parents' wishes.
> The ladies' hats.

An " s " is added if the plural does not end in that letter, and is preceded by the apostrophe.

> The children's ward.
> Women's rights.

(*b*) When single letters are used as words, the apostrophe is inserted before the " s " of the plural.

> He knows how to watch his p's and q's.

(*c*) The apostrophe is used to denote that some letter or letters of a word are omitted.

> Can't (cannot); don't (do not); 'phone (telephone).

It is not necessary to insert an apostrophe when a word contracted in the middle is pronounced as if it were written in full. " Dr." is an example. If the contraction is at the end of the word, the apostrophe must be used, e.g., Middlesboro'.

ITALICS

(*a*) ITALICS are used to give emphasis.

It was *the* event of the season.

(*b*) Foreign words and phrases are printed in italics.

The action was held to be *ultra vires*.

He was a master of the *bon mot*.

This rule does not apply to foreign words that have been incorporated in the English language. Examples:—

Charabanc, incognito, restaurant, menu, revue.

(*c*) Names of newspapers and ships are usually printed in italics ; titles of books and other forms of composition may also be italicised.

Italics are indicated for the printer by drawing a line under the word or words to be italicised.

MARKS OF ELLIPSIS

(*a*) WHEN words are left out in the middle of a quotation, the omission—which is called an ellipsis—is marked by placing several full stops in a line. Formerly asterisks were employed for this purpose, but are now rarely used.

> The report stated: "The past year has been one of exceptional activity. . . . It is hoped that this progress will be maintained."

(*b*) When only the initial letter of a name is given, a dash is added to mark the omission of the remaining letters.

I had a letter yesterday from J—, who has been staying at C—— for some weeks.

The length of the dash is usually determined by the number of letters omitted.

HOW TO PUNCTUATE A LETTER

ERRORS in the punctuation of letters are so frequently made as to justify a detailed explanation of the standard practice.

The address should be written as follows :—

> Mr. A. Brown,
> 10, High Street,
> Whitetown.

Another form :—

> A. Brown, Esq., J.P.,
> 10, High St.,
> Whitetown.

Esq. and J.P. take the full stop because they are abbreviations. Note that a comma separates Esq. from J.P., and that a comma marks the end of the line (or part of the name and address), as in the first example. Similarly, " St." is followed by a full stop to mark the abbreviation and a comma because it ends the line (but not the address). If the name only is given at the head or the foot of a letter, a full stop should be placed after it to denote completion.

The date may be written in either of the following ways :—

November 28th, 1924.
28th November, 1924.

"Dear Sir ", "Dear Sirs" or "Gentlemen" should be followed by a comma, and the letter proper should begin slightly to the right on the line below.

The correct punctuation of the complimentary close is shown by the following examples :—

    Yours faithfully,

    I am,
        Yours sincerely,

    I have the honour to remain,
        Your obedient servant,

THE USE OF CAPITAL LETTERS

THE following need capital letters :—

The first word in a sentence or a line of verse.

The pronoun I.

Names and pronouns referring to the Deity, e.g., the Maker, He, Him.

Proper nouns, e.g., Henry Brown.

Religious denominations—Wesleyan, Primitive Methodist, etc.

Political parties—Conservative, Liberal, Socialist, etc.

Days of the week and months of the year.

Festivals, e.g., Easter, Christmas.

Principal words in the titles of books, plays, etc. Example : " The Last of the Barons."

Names of specific rulers—the King of England, the President of France, etc.

Names of specific societies, clubs, buildings, streets, etc.

Names of notable events, e.g., the Armistice.

GEORGE ALLEN & UNWIN LTD

Head Office:
London: 40 Museum Street, W.C.1.

Trade orders and enquiries
Park Lane, Hemel Hempstead, Herts.

Auckland: P.O. Box 36012, Northcote Central N.4
Barbados: P.O. Box 222, Bridgetown
Bombay: 15 Graham Road, Ballard Estate, Bombay 1
Buenos Aires: Escritorio 454-459, Florida 165
Beirut: Deeb Building, Jeanne d'Arc Street
Calcutta: 17 Chittaranjan Avenue, Calcutta 13
Cape Town: 68 Shortmarket Street
Hong Kong: 105 Wing On Mansion, 26 Hancow Road, Kowloon
Ibadan: P.O. Box 62
Karachi: Karachi Chambers, McLeod Road
Madras: Mohan Mansions, 38c Mount Road, Madras 6
Mexico: Villalongin 32, Mexico 5, D.F.
Nairobi: P.O. Box 30583
New Delhi: 13-14 Asaf Ali Road, New Delhi 1
Ontario: 81 Curlew Drive, Don Mills
Philippines: P.O. Box 157, Quezon City D.502
Rio de Janeiro: Caixa Postal 2537-Zc-00
Singapore: 36c Prinsep Street, Singapore 7
Sydney N.S.W.: Bradbury House, 55 York Street
Tokyo: P.O. Box 26, Kamata

by Harold Herd
WATCH YOUR ENGLISH

by John Rigg
HOW TO CONDUCT A MEETING

'Should be invaluable. It is a protection against ignorance and abstraction.' DAILY HERALD

HOW TO TAKE THE CHAIR

'A comprehensive guide to the duties of chairman. The section on amendments will be found particularly lucid and helpful.'
BIRMINGHAM GAZETTE

PLATFORM ORATORY AND DEBATE

Thirty years' experience of public speaking have gone to the making of this eminently practical little book.

by Beryl Heitland
HOW TO WRITE GOOD LETTERS

GEORGE ALLEN & UNWIN LTD